MAJOR SPORTS EVENTS

THE WORLD SERIES

BY HUBERT WALKER

WWW.APEXEDITIONS.COM

Copyright © 2023 by Apex Editions, Mendota Heights, MN 55120. All rights reserved. No part of this book may be reproduced or utilized in any form or by any means without written permission from the publisher.

Apex is distributed by North Star Editions:
sales@northstareditions.com | 888-417-0195

Produced for Apex by Red Line Editorial.

Photographs ©: Eric Gay/AP Images, cover; Jim Mone/AP Images, 1, 22–23; Sue Ogrocki/AP Images, 4–5; Shutterstock Images, 6–7, 18, 20–21; David J. Phillip/AP Images, 8–9; Bain News Service/Library of Congress, 10–11, 14–15; AP Images, 12–13; National Photo Company Collection/Library of Congress, 15; Adam Hunger/AP Images, 16–17; Hans Deryk/AP Images, 19; Mark Duncan/AP Images, 24–25, 29; Charlie Riedel/AP Images, 26–27

Library of Congress Control Number: 2022912064

ISBN
978-1-63738-297-4 (hardcover)
978-1-63738-333-9 (paperback)
978-1-63738-403-9 (ebook pdf)
978-1-63738-369-8 (hosted ebook)

Printed in the United States of America
Mankato, MN
012023

NOTE TO PARENTS AND EDUCATORS

Apex books are designed to build literacy skills in striving readers. Exciting, high-interest content attracts and holds readers' attention. The text is carefully leveled to allow students to achieve success quickly. Additional features, such as bolded glossary words for difficult terms, help build comprehension.

TABLE OF CONTENTS

CHAPTER 1
THE FALL CLASSIC 4

CHAPTER 2
WORLD SERIES HISTORY 10

CHAPTER 3
PATH TO THE WORLD SERIES 16

CHAPTER 4
MAGICAL MOMENTS 22

COMPREHENSION QUESTIONS • 28
GLOSSARY • 30
TO LEARN MORE • 31
ABOUT THE AUTHOR • 31
INDEX • 32

CHAPTER 1

THE FALL CLASSIC

The batter takes a powerful swing. He hits the ball deep to left field. The ball sails over the fence. It's a home run!

Atlanta Braves player Jorge Soler blasts a three-run home run during the 2021 World Series.

The Atlanta Braves are facing the Houston Astros. It's Game 6 of the 2021 World Series. The Braves lead the series three games to two.

FAST FACT

The World Series is known as the Fall Classic.

Game 6 of the 2021 World Series took place at Minute Maid Park in Houston, Texas.

Braves catcher Travis d'Arnaud and pitcher Will Smith celebrate after winning the 2021 World Series.

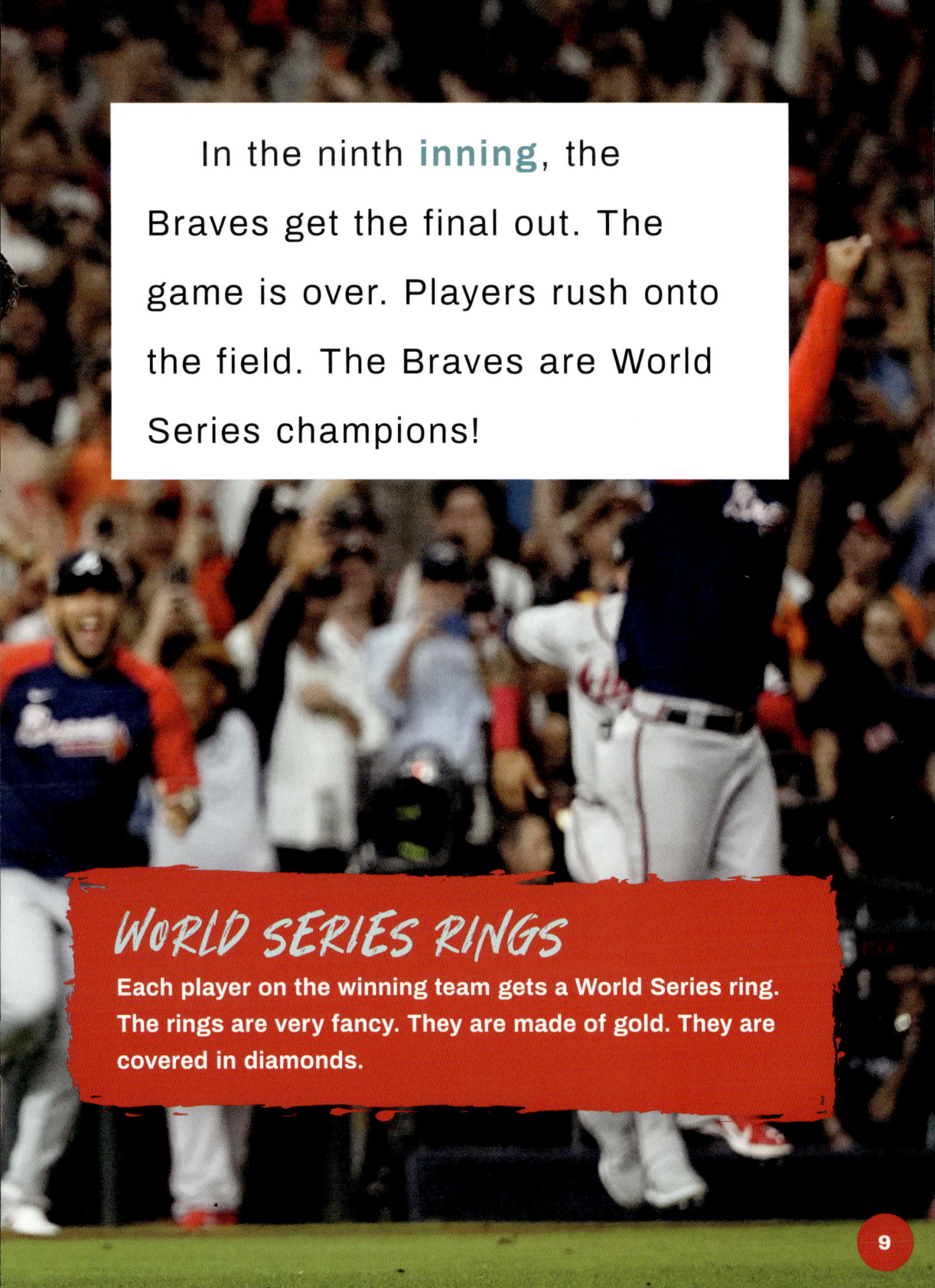

In the ninth **inning**, the Braves get the final out. The game is over. Players rush onto the field. The Braves are World Series champions!

WORLD SERIES RINGS

Each player on the winning team gets a World Series ring. The rings are very fancy. They are made of gold. They are covered in diamonds.

CHAPTER 2

WORLD SERIES HISTORY

Professional baseball started in the 1800s. By the early 1900s, there were two major **leagues**. One was the National League (NL). The other was the American League (AL).

Cy Young's pitching helped Boston win the first World Series in 1903.

So many fans went to Game 3 of the first World Series in 1903 that they overflowed onto the field.

Each league had a champion in 1903. These two teams played against each other. It was the first World Series.

THE BOSTON AMERICANS

In 1903, the Boston Americans won the first World Series. They defeated the Pittsburgh Pirates. Today, Boston's team is known as the Red Sox.

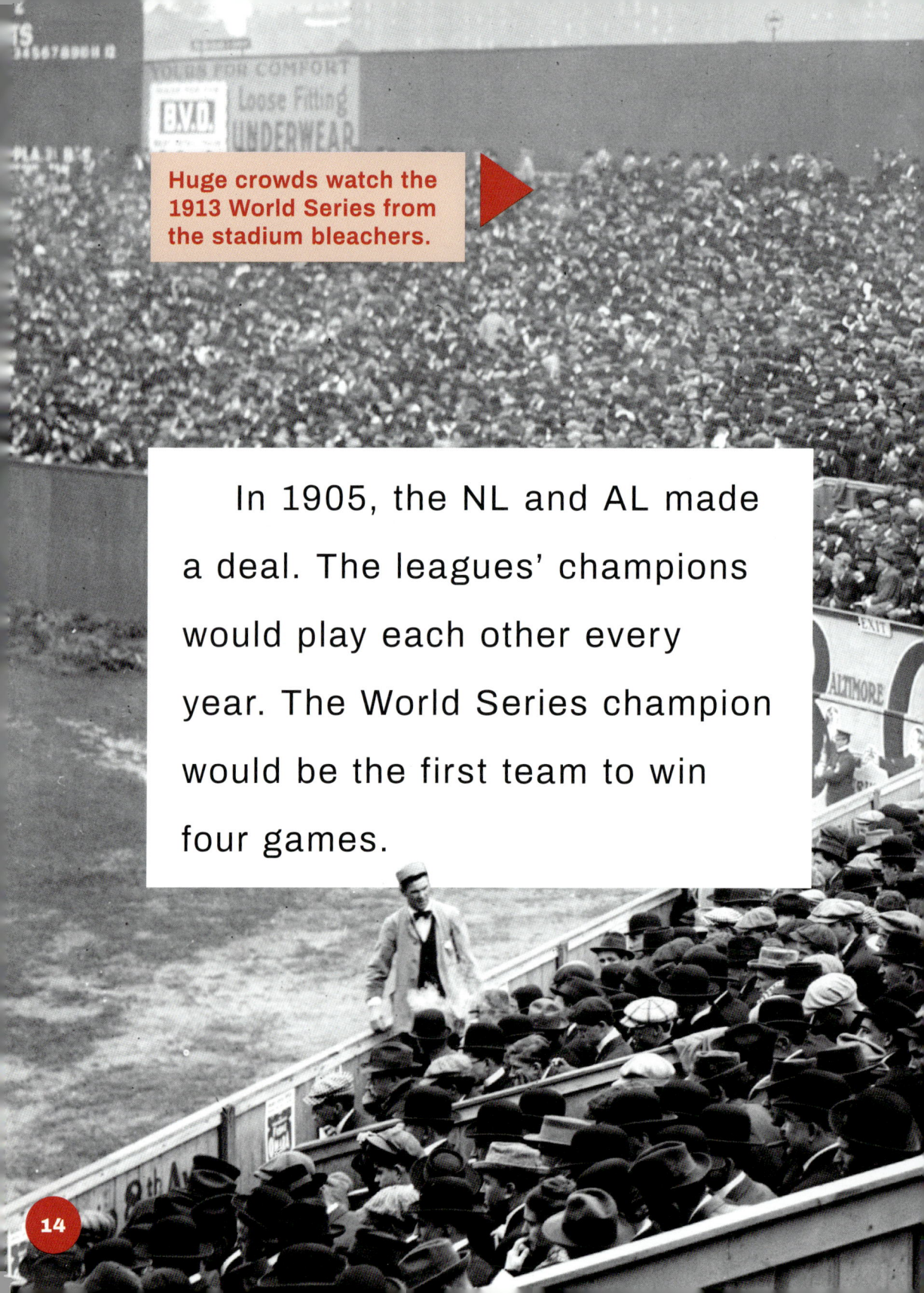

Huge crowds watch the 1913 World Series from the stadium bleachers.

In 1905, the NL and AL made a deal. The leagues' champions would play each other every year. The World Series champion would be the first team to win four games.

FAST FACT
From 1949 to 1953, the New York Yankees won five straight World Series.

A Washington Senators player slides into second base during the 1925 World Series.

CHAPTER 3

PATH TO THE WORLD SERIES

Each league has three **divisions**. Each division has five teams. The winner of each division reaches the **postseason**.

In 2021, the Tampa Bay Rays won the AL East division.

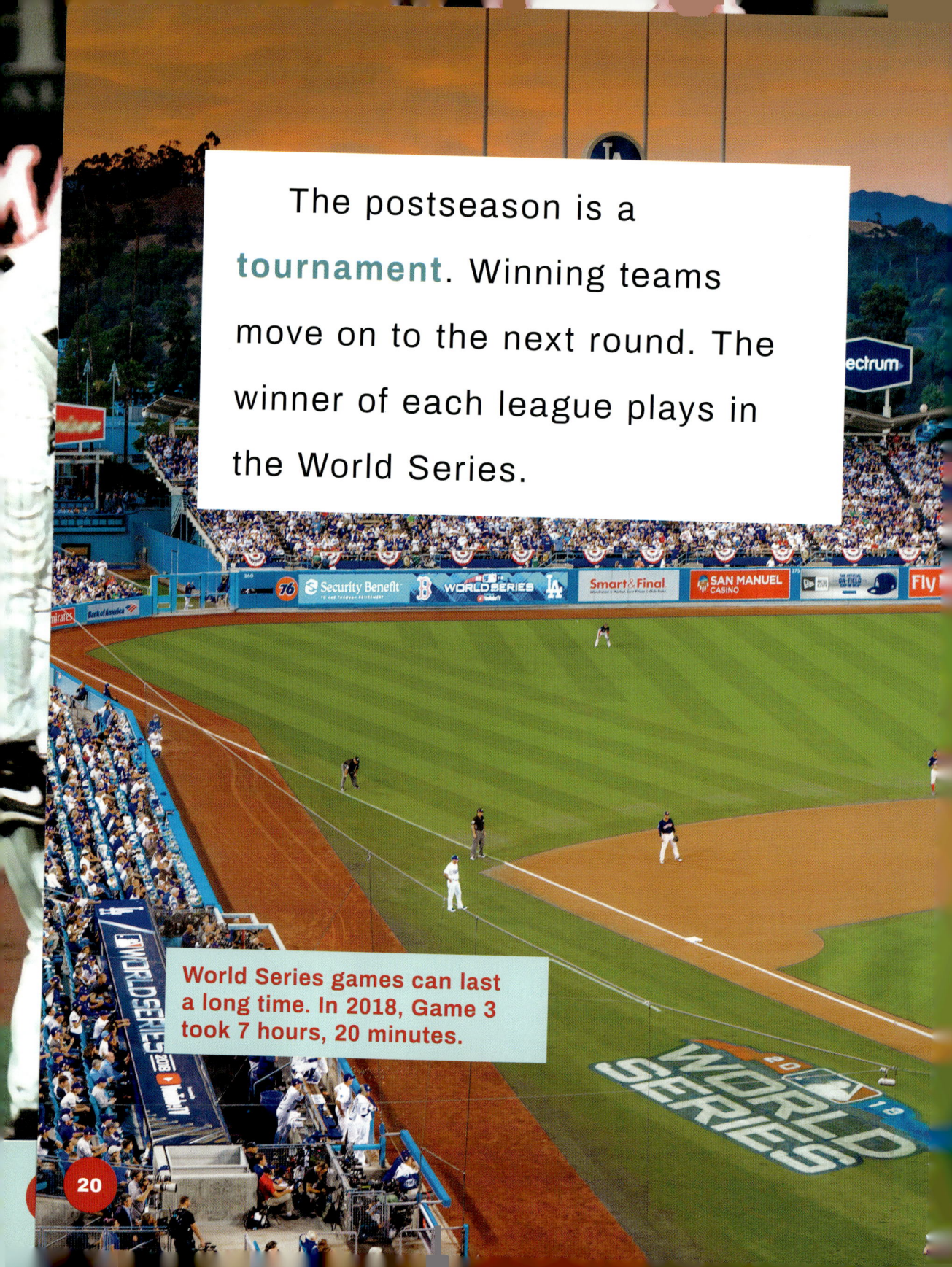

The postseason is a **tournament**. Winning teams move on to the next round. The winner of each league plays in the World Series.

World Series games can last a long time. In 2018, Game 3 took 7 hours, 20 minutes.

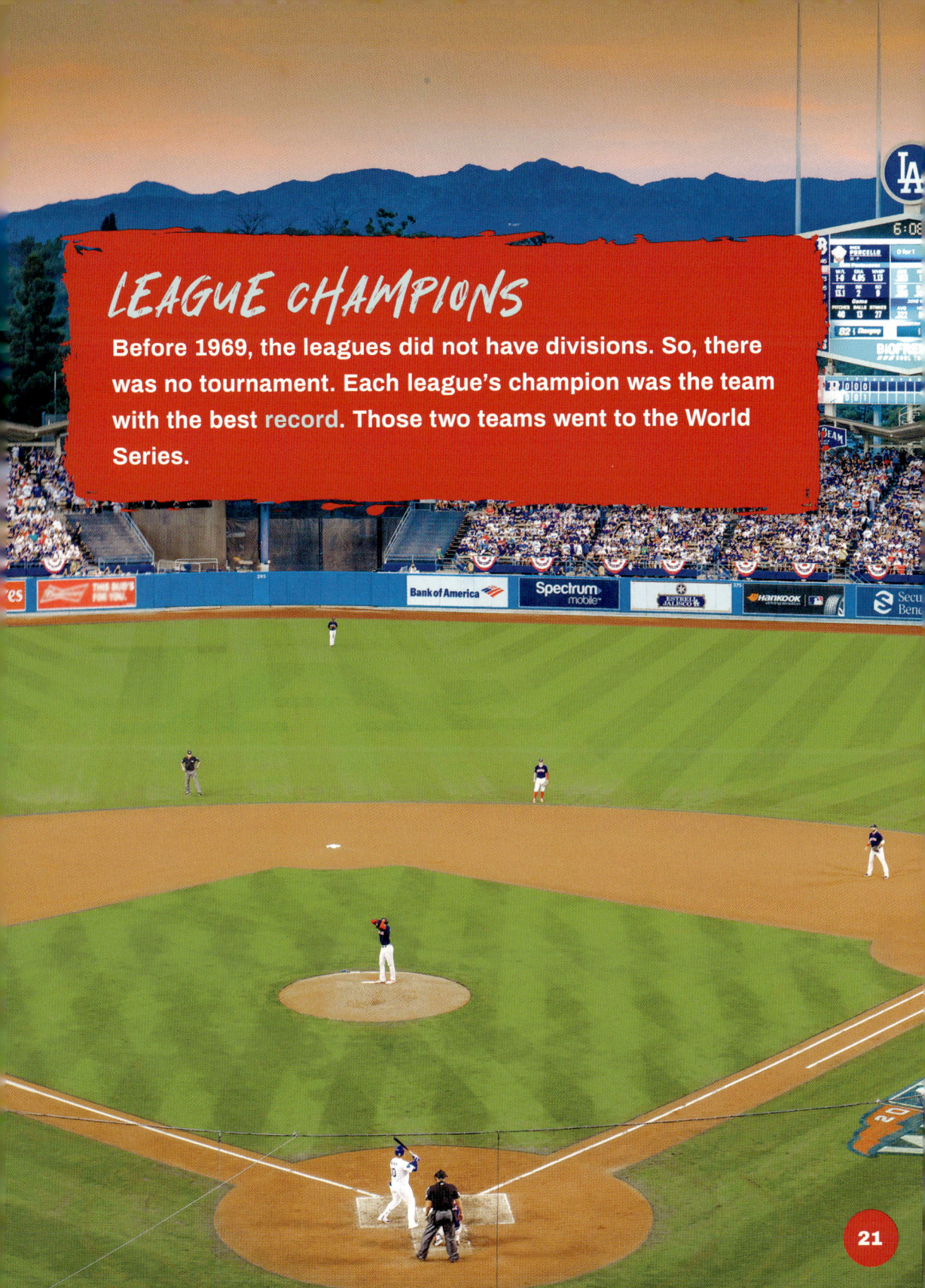

LEAGUE CHAMPIONS

Before 1969, the leagues did not have divisions. So, there was no tournament. Each league's champion was the team with the best record. Those two teams went to the World Series.

CHAPTER 4

MAGICAL MOMENTS

The 1991 World Series came down to Game 7. The score was tied 0–0 after nine innings. The Minnesota Twins won in the tenth inning.

Jack Morris pitched 10 scoreless innings in Game 7 of the 1991 World Series.

Joe Carter celebrates after hitting a World-Series-winning home run.

In 1993, the Toronto Blue Jays trailed in Game 6. Then Joe Carter homered in the ninth inning. The Blue Jays were champions.

FAST FACT

There was no World Series in 1994. The players were on **strike** that year.

NEW YORK YANKEES

No team has won the World Series more times than the New York Yankees. As of 2021, the Yankees had 27 World Series titles.

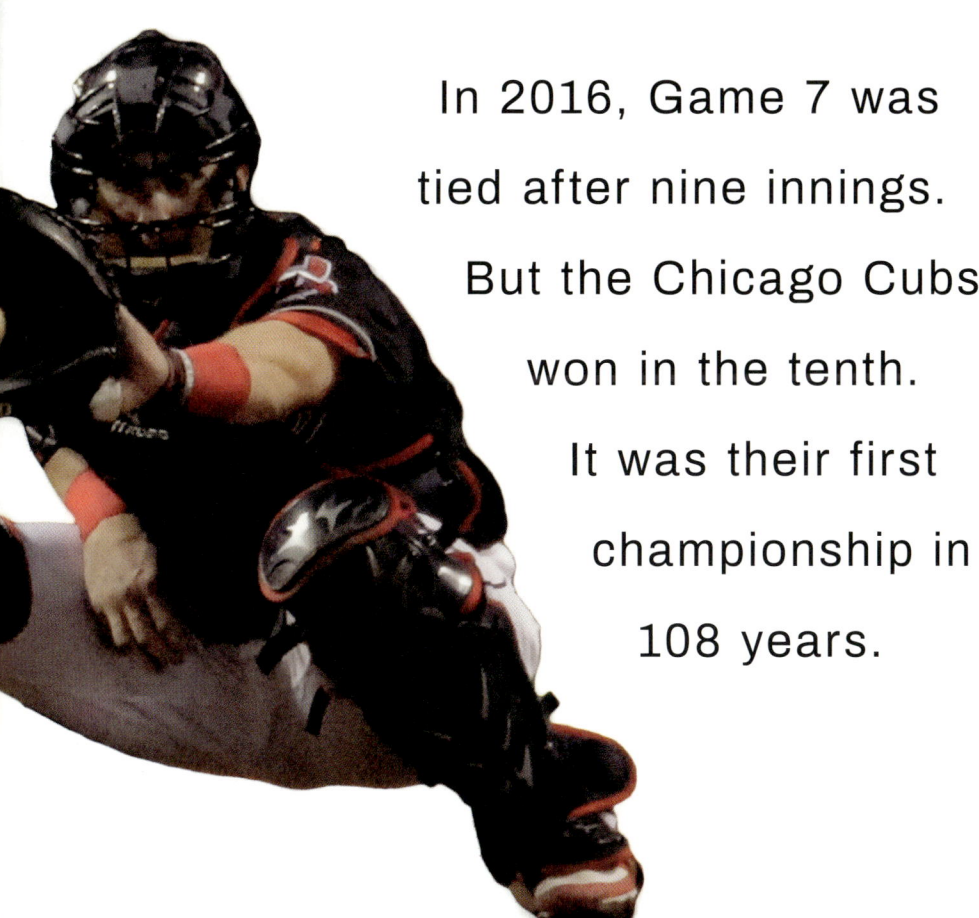

In 2016, Game 7 was tied after nine innings. But the Chicago Cubs won in the tenth. It was their first championship in 108 years.

Ben Zobrist hits a double for the Cubs during Game 7 of the 2016 World Series.

COMPREHENSION QUESTIONS

Write your answers on a separate piece of paper.

1. Write a paragraph that explains the main ideas of Chapter 3.

2. Do you think the postseason should include wild-card teams? Why or why not?

3. The Chicago Cubs' 2016 World Series title was their first win in how many years?

    A. 3
    B. 49
    C. 108

4. How can a team reach the postseason if the team does not win its division?

    A. It can join a different league.
    B. It can be a wild-card team.
    C. It can lose most of its games.

5. What does **defeated** mean in this book?

In 1903, the Boston Americans won the first World Series. They defeated the Pittsburgh Pirates.

    A. tied
    B. beat
    C. lost to

6. What does **titles** mean in this book?

No team has won the World Series more times than the New York Yankees. As of 2021, the Yankees had 27 World Series titles.

    A. stories from long ago
    B. names of books
    C. championship wins

Answer key on page 32.

GLOSSARY

divisions
Groups of teams within a league.

inning
Part of a baseball game. A regular baseball game has nine innings. More innings are added if the game is tied.

leagues
Groups of teams that play one another.

postseason
A set of games played after the regular season to decide which team will be the champion.

professional
Having to do with people who get paid for what they do.

record
The wins and losses that a team has during a season.

strike
When people stop working as a way to demand better pay or better working conditions.

tournament
A competition that includes several teams.

BOOKS

Abdo, Kenny. *Miracle Moments in Baseball*. Minneapolis: Abdo Publishing, 2022.

Fishman, Jon M. *Baseball's G.O.A.T.: Babe Ruth, Mike Trout, and More*. Minneapolis: Lerner Publications, 2020.

Hewson, Anthony K. *Baseball Records*. Lake Elmo, MN: Focus Readers, 2021.

ONLINE RESOURCES

Visit **www.apexeditions.com** to find links and resources related to this title.

ABOUT THE AUTHOR

Hubert Walker enjoys running, hunting, and going to the dog park with his best pal. He grew up in Georgia but moved to Minnesota in 2018.

INDEX

A
American League (AL), 10, 14
Atlanta Braves, 7, 9

B
Boston Red Sox, 13

C
Carter, Joe, 25
Chicago Cubs, 27

D
divisions, 16, 19, 21

F
Florida Marlins, 18

H
Houston Astros, 7

M
Minnesota Twins, 22

N
National League (NL), 10, 14
New York Yankees, 15, 27

P
Pittsburgh Pirates, 13
postseason, 16, 19–20

T
Toronto Blue Jays, 25

W
wild-card teams, 18–19
World Series rings, 9

ANSWER KEY:
1. Answers will vary; 2. Answers will vary; 3. C; 4. B; 5. B; 6. C